Reaching the Essence of Development

A Chapbook & Journal

For Teen Girls defining Strength, Courage & Wisdom!

A compilation of Letters, Poetry, Scriptures, Quotes
and Advice for the Teen Soul

Written in By Tracie Berry-McGhee, M.Ed., LPC

&

N.i.a Sisters

(Collective works from Women dedicated to
Nurturing Inner Awareness)

Dedicated to my Teen SistaKeepers!
Reaching their Essence of Development

Mentally, Spiritually & Physically

In honor of

JaMeah Echols

(March 9. 1991- June 22. 2009)

Nurturing Inner Awareness...

SistaKeeper Mission & Vision

Vision

SistaKeeper empowers young women to be inspired to develop their mind, body & spirit into women with a strong sense of self and purpose, dedicated to making a difference in the lives of themselves, and their community.

Mission

SistaKeeper creates a society of young women who know who they are, what they believe in, and what they stand for. They can make educated choices, be assertive, display teamwork and be true to self, fighting for issues that plague our communities, thus, becoming cycle breakers.

Reaching the Essence of Development

Developed to Nurture, Inspire & Empower

Foreword

When SistaKeeper started in 2002 in my basement, I knew God was planting seeds for many young girls to grow into Soulflowers that would indeed birth a nation of change. This is what mentoring is all about, circles for girls that inspire us to be keepers. It is so crucial that we all know that no one can save the universe but I felt if I could just make a difference in the life of one young lady, so be it! Many women birthed words of wisdom into me and for that I am forever grateful!

Yes my mother was a teen mom, perfect? No, but she was the best mother she could be and she was mine! She taught me to write, read and best of all to dream and she taught me to be a keeper!

My mom has many female friends that were a part of her village and she was a support to them, that is what a keeper is, your village.

Our SistaKeeper village began with seven young girls, and I kept in touch with them all. They are all on the journey to womanhood now, successfully defining their destiny. As you continue to reflect on what is next in your life, I wanted to share with you a glimpse of what 1 of the 7 girls had to say when I contacted her to see if she remembered her SistaKeeper experience.

I asked her 3 questions:

1. Do you remember the first circle?

2. What do you remember?

3. What are you doing now & did SistaKeeper make a difference?

Oh yes, *A Sista Keeper is You, A SistaKeeper is Me, a Sista Keeper is We! Uh Uh, I definitely remember.*
It was one of life's defining moments for me because it made me think about what it meant to be a girl. Growing up, I was the little girl that didn't like girly stuff, and in a household where males dominated, it was easy for me to want to do what my brothers did. I would complain about wearing dresses, and being dainty. I got embarrassed when people called me pretty. My elementary school friends loved lip smackers chapstick and lip gloss, and I was like "Nope, I don't need that."

Yeah, I was a mess... But I remember sitting in Mrs. McGhee's basement on blow up cushions and beanbag chairs in a circle as she passed out journals and pens with flowers on top and she gave us a poem to read out loud. They were affirmations about who we were and who we were free to be. She taught us that we were all beautiful despite what others said about us and she asked us what we each thought beauty was. Of course each of us answered differently, I just remember that she said beauty was more than what was on the outside. And that beauty comes in different forms, and the outside should reflect what's on the inside.

I remember she told us to write in our journals every day; write what we felt, write poems, songs, and whatever else came to mind. She told us the power of self-expression, and how not to be afraid of ourselves. That it all depended on what we thought of ourselves and not what others thought of us. At age 11, this was exactly what I needed to hear. I was pretty much hooked with Sista Keeper after that first day and I can recall many different experiences with Mrs. McGhee, her daughters and all the other Sistas. And to this day, I still write all the time, I don't worry about what others think of me but I express myself in ways that I want to and I do what makes me happy.

As of now, I am attending Claflin University, a small Methodist affiliated HBCU in Orangeburg, South Carolina on a full ride scholarship. In May 2014, I will be graduating with a

B.S. degree in Biology, and I am making plans to pursue a Master's Degree in Public Health, with a concentration in Community Health and Prevention. In the last few years, I co-founded an organization called Sisters of Service on my college campus, which is a community service organization for Christian women; and I also co-founded an organization called PRESS LLC (Powerful Resilience Empowering Strong Sisterhood) with my mother and sister, which is a women empowerment organization. I have just had my first study abroad experience in India, which was both eye opening and life changing, and I have been in the process of learning Hindi. My life aspirations are to open a Community Health Center, become a Family Physician, and publish Christian Fiction for Young Adults. Overall I am simply Trusting God on this Life Journey, and thanking Him for making me who I am, allowing me to have wonderful people like Mrs. McGhee in my life and letting me know that I can do ALL THINGS through HIM, who gives me strength.

With that being said, SistaKeeper did indeed make a difference. Anything that lets a girl know that it is okay to be herself opens up the doors to self-confidence, self-awareness, and self-empowerment, helping her realize that SHE IS, SHE CAN, and SHE WILL, in a world that is constantly saying she is not and she cannot.
Thanks and God Bless,
Love, Presh (Precious Crittenden)

With that being said, I am on a mission with the help of Nia Sisters, encouraging you to define your destiny, Reaching the Essence of your Development. Take the pledge, Free Yo Mind and Begin your walk of Faith! Knowing you too are a Keeper!

SistaKeeper Pledge!

I am who I am
I am unique
I am We
I represent Unity!

I am diversity
A mosaic of people live in me
I am my history
My story is my legacy!

My voice delivers solutions
My mind seeks knowledge
My spirit flows with purpose!

I am inspired
I am empowered
I am naturally me!

I reflect positivity
I hold the key to my destiny
It's all about me!

I Define Me!

Hey Lil Sista,

Young and bright!

What are your wishes? What is your fight? What are your dreams, desires, destiny? What speaks to your heart?

Do you know you will be alright? GOD has a plan for you and it is time for you to free your mind & take flight!

This RED book & journal is just for you!

Enjoy a collection of letters, poems and affirmations. This will be like being in a circle, you get to "free yo mind!" get the answers to "what you want to know", while your Nia Sisters (Keepers) sit on the "hot seat" and share their advice.

A Keeper is a woman known as your Nia Sisters. Nia means "purpose" in Swahili and these women of purpose share their letters of advice gifting you with the tools to inspire you to find your special gifts.

Be a Keeper to thyself and know you have all the tools within will help to get you through! We are just here to push you!

RED means **Reaching your Essence of Development**.

Allow your developmental process to begin, as you turn the pages sow seeds into yourself, read & read again, reflect, journal and create chapters that begin and end with you…

This is your RED Book. Know that you are a Keeper, you define you and you will find your purpose when you begin to Nurture Inner Awareness! Be Empowe(red),

Your SistaKeeper,

Tracie Berry-McGhee, M.Ed. LPC (DivineTea)

Table of Contents

Free Yo Mind! (Poetry)

What I Want to Know?

Hot Seat (letters from a Nia Sista)

Little girls are to be seen and not heard!

True or false

False… because you are a RED girl! You are to always be seen but for the right things. Act like a lady, walking with authority, sitting with poise, standing alone if necessary. As long as you know you are worthy to be known. You are always to be heard but for speaking positive words that show the world you have a voice that empowers!

As a RED girl, entering into womanhood know you have a responsibility to carry a torch of walking the walk and talking the talk! Little girls are watching you and you must know from the start that you are Reaching the Essence of Development, SO be seen and be heard but for the right things and remember you are a RED girl, thus a SistaKeeper for life!

LISTEN, LISTEN, LISTEN

Dress well this morning

We have places to go,

Rise up from your bed

Make haste don't be slow,

Put on Kindness, Humility,

And yes wear that too,

That is Truth,

It should cover all that you do.

Get up now get moving

We do need to fly,

I will lift you till your

Fingers touch the

Edge of the sky.

No, remove that, uh-uh

Don't wear that Anxiety and Worry,

Take that off, there's no time,

We do need to hurry.

A storm's coming, grab that

Alertness and Sobriety too,

There are beasts in the storm, but I will protect you.

Just remember to stand

Resistant and Firm,

Pull my armor around you,

You are not alone!

Yes, the trouble will come,

I won't lie – it will hurt you,

But I promise you, I will never,

Never desert you.

And this place we are going,

Child, you just wait - I will take you,

Where all things are new and,

You may rest and grow stronger,

Where Peace and Grace live,

And Love is around you.

Just grip to my hand,

I am Strong

And I am True,

And above everything else,

I'll ALWAYS love you!
Based on 1 PETER 5:5-10,

By Madeline Jackson

DO as I say and Not as I do?

True or False?

False, as a woman your word means everything and your actions speak to which direction you will take. So seek knowledge first before moving on impulse. Be still as you meditate to determine your next steps. Remember, unfortunately family and friends may turn on you, because they sometimes do, but GOD will always have your back and that my darling will always be True!

YES!

Yes,

The shoe will drop

The sky will fall

The earth will be pulled out from under your feet

Your heart will be broken

But before that happens

You will dance barefoot with yourself

Twirl in the nakedness

Authenticity brings

You will kiss the sky

grasp clouds in your palm

Dream wildly of constellations and stars

Your roots will reach

tenderly

Fearlessly into dark places

Pushed forward

by life and calls of creation

And your heart

Your tenacious, fragile heart

Will always choose love

Will always willingly plunge

In the red river of living

Knowing all the while

the worst that can happen

is the inevitable

that the shoe will still drop

The sky will still fall

Your heart will likely get broken

Again

and again

Oh that you would be so lucky

Because it is everything that comes before

That makes all that follows

Easier to bare.

By Elizabeth Vega

Dear little Sista,

Words cannot begin to express how extremely proud of you I am for making it this far. This is only the beginning so that means there is so much more in store for you. I want to give you a few pieces of advice that are helping me on this journey called life.

1. "It's not the critic who counts"

Believe me when I say you won't be able to make everyone happy all the time. Whenever you give an idea, a creative piece, or even blood, sweat, and tears, there will always be someone trying to tear you down. However, for every one person attempting to tear you down there are at least five or six people there to lift you up...some you may not even know. Don't let the fear of rejection and criticism keep you from living and succeeding.

2. "Be You"

What are the chances that out of millions of sperm and eggs you would be chosen--that's no accident; due to you being chosen you possess certain unique talents, personality traits, and gifts...use them and BE YOU! Even Dr. Seuss recognized the importance of individuality when he said, "Today you are you. That is truer than you. There is no one alive who is more you than you."

3. Do everything from a place of "love".

Now when I say love, I don't mean from a romantic standpoint. I mean a standpoint of, "I want what's best for you and you want what's best for me." There are millions of hurt souls wandering around this planet just looking for someone to say or show, "I care." Whenever you talk with someone from a place of love you are single handedly healing the world one person at a time." Everything starts with love.

My dear little sister I hope these life lessons help you through your darkest moments, for it is when it's darkest that our souls shine the brightest.

Yours in love and light,
Aleshia Patterson

Dear Sister,

I sit here wondering what to say to you. I'll start off by saying that you are strong, powerful and wonderfully awesome. I'll also tell you that I love you. I must say that I couldn't always say that because I really didn't know what love was.

Sure I love my kids, my folks and my family but it is hard to love someone else when you don't have love for yourself first. Throughout my life I have been many things that I am not so proud of, all due to the perceptions I had of myself.

All my life I've felt like an outsider to my family, my friends and my life. Because of those feelings I have always bent over backwards for people. People pleasing, it is called "wanting to be liked, loved or just to fit in and I was willing to do almost anything. You get the point. I did have one good friend, surprisingly we are still friends to this day.

Feeling unloved led me to looking for love in all the wrong places, with wrong people, doing wrong things. My search for love should have started with the Creator, recognizing how much he loved and sacrificed for me. 2nd place I should have looked was within, seeing how fabulous I am. Yet my journey led to teen pregnancy and by the time I was 22, I had 4 kids by three different guys. I married one of them, but really didn't love him. I had created a mess of my own making, no healthy choices.

I was hard headed and stubborn and didn't want to see the truth right in front of me. I say this to say my challenge to you is to be smart, use your head and do the right thing and think about your future daily. Meet that challenge head on. It won't be sunshine and roses every day. There will be showers and storms but it will not rain forever. Rainbows follow the storms, as for me I am now enjoying marching to my own beat in my own parade with a banner that says "It is all about me!" because I have learned to truly love myself and lil sista I love you too!

Love,

Big Sis Tonya

Define why you love yourself?

_____
_____
_____
_____
_____
_____
_____
_____
_____
_____
_____
_____
_____
_____

Cleansing my Body- Hygiene 101

Face Care: As you are growing your face may be oily or dry. So you need to get a technique that you like. I love the simple technique of hot water first (as hot as you can get it) it opens your pores to clean out the dirt. Then follow up with a cold towel to close the pores up. If you suffer from acne, it is best to talk to a dermatologist for advice.

Showers & baths: It's your body, but you live in a world with people who will tell you if you fresh or not so clean. So I thought we might want to go over the basics. I know you are saying I know these things. Well maybe, but just in case let us cover all bases. Showers should occur daily, or at least every other day. When you were a little girl, you didn't have to take as many showers, but now you might notice that if you skip a day or two, your body odor may start to get to you. This is because you are at the age that your body is constantly going through changes that make it necessary for you to pay extra close attention to your hygiene, and that means taking showers or baths. In the shower, clean yourself with soap and water. Changes going on in your sweat and oil glands make it especially important for you to keep yourself fresh and clean. Now you don't have to smell like wildflowers but you must use soap or your favorite body wash. Be careful though, your skin may be sensitive different scents and lotions. Washing yourself with a good, mild soap will help cut down on body odor by attacking bacteria that might make the smell worse. Always, always bathe first before applying deodorant next.

Deodorant & antiperspirant: If you are tripping out about the sweat and smell factor, relax. That's what deodorant and antiperspirant are there for. Antiperspirant is used to stop sweating by drying up your sweat glands. Deodorant masks the smell with a "pretty" fragrance, like baby powder or flowers. You can find a combination of both antiperspirant and deodorant in one product, which works very well. When you first begin using deodorant, you might want to try different brands to see which one works best for you. You can also keep body wipes with you, if you feel you need a little extra support.

Hair care: During puberty, it may seem like everything in your body is changing, even your hair! Perhaps your hair and your scalp feel oily, and you have to wash your hair more often. This is all part of your body's hormonal changes—the same thing that causes acne.

All girls have different types of hair, so there isn't one way to care for it. Some girls desire to cold wash their hair daily or you may choose less frequently— depends on if your scalp is dry or oily. This is based on genetics, something that you can't control. Girls of different ethnicities have different concerns regarding hair care, so be sure to pick a washing routine and hair care products that work best for you (not what your friend or your favorite celebrity uses). It is easy to become a product junkie so remember just because it is expensive doesn't mean it's the best and just because it says it works on the label doesn't mean it will work for you.

Douching, shaving, panty liners and such: By now, I am sure you are about to enter the menses stages of your life. Cycles that comes periodically or monthly. We must try to stay as fresh and comfortable as possible. So do your research on products that work for you, some have wings, and a variety of shapes and sizes, but this is about your preference, after all it is your body. A bit of advice, cotton panties help your vaginal area to breathe, pantyliners are a daily recommendation for those of you with normal discharges because they keep you covered from stains and odors. I would stay away from scented pads and tampons is a personal choice, just know if you choose them, change them often. As for douching again, your body really can take of itself, you don't need wildflower scents in your insides, if you must a little vinegar in your bathwater will do the trick. As for shaving you've probably noticed all that hair growing on your body in different places. If you want to shave, talk with your mother or a trusted adult to get her advice. There are special brands for sensitive skin. You should also find an easy-to-use razor, lotion, cream or gel that you feel comfortable controlling. When you start to shave, pull from the foot up for the best results. Be careful around your knee and ankle, where the skin is bumpier and it's easy to cut yourself. If you do happen to cut yourself, don't be alarmed. The blood comes very fast in shaving accidents. Put a band-aid on after you dry your leg to help stop the bleeding. If you're concerned about hair in other places, again, it is all about personal preference so talk to an adult or your mentor. Be careful with these procedures because you could seriously irritate your skin.

RED Girls are always clean inside and out! So grab your RED bag and begin to fill it up!

CREATE a list of personal hygiene items that are a **Necessity** for your RED bag needs:

_____

_____

_____

Dear Little Sis,

You were created by God to be unique and wonderful just the way you are. There has never been and will never be another you. I know sometimes it is not easy because people will try to make you feel like there is something wrong with you. When you watch TV the advertisers show products that encourage you to be different. The same thing happened to me when I was in middle school. I did not understand my worth.

When I was in the 5th grade I was five feet eight inches tall. Kids and many of my teachers literally looked up to me. I would always have to be the last person in line when we lined up from shortest to tallest. To make matter worse I really felt uncomfortable being me. Many kids would joke about my size and some days I wished I could just shrink and be the same as everyone else.

I am not sure if you feel that way about some area of your life, but I am writing to you today to let you know , little sis, you are fabulous just the way you are. My mother would always tell me that I am beautiful and to walk with my head held high. Even though I didn't always want to do that and it didn't feel comfortable I tried my best to take her advice and find something that made me feel confident. It wasn't easy, but everything changed for me when I started playing basketball my first love.

Basketball changed my life because it provided the space for me to learn something new, develop friendships and experience success.

Despite how much I enjoyed playing it was very difficult in the beginning because I did not know all of the technical aspects of the game. Nevertheless I kept listening to my coaches and trying to do what they asked and it all worked out.

I eventually received a full scholarship to Saint Louis University and played in Germany. Also, there were so many other tall girls who played basketball that I felt right at home and not like an alien. Over the years my teammates became some of my best friends since we had something we loved in common.

Little sis, my purpose of telling you about my journey with basketball is simply to encourage you to explore different activities and find something you enjoy. Everyone is blessed with unique gifts and talents that we simply have to find.

Perhaps you love music and play an instrument or sing. Maybe, you are great at Lego Robotics and enjoy programming. Possibly, you are a gifted artist who enjoys drawing or theatre. Whatever your gift, interest or talent put your heart into it and learn as much as possible. When you nurture your gifts they blossom and you are eager to share your gifts with others.

My beautiful, brilliant, bold, blessed little sister. There has never been and will never be another you! Walk with you head held high, trust that little voice inside of you leading you in the right direction and always honor yourself as a queen. The world is ready for you to share your gifts!

With all the love my heart can hold,

Coach Angie Lewis

Ode to a Little Sis

Your life is indeed your life, take care of it.

Your body is yours alone,

Nurture it.

Your mind can only be moved by you,

Educate it.

Your soul breathes through you,

Enlighten it.

You only get one shot at this thing called LIFE.

Live every minute as if you'd want to exist in this moment in history
with pride, appreciation and educated wisdom.

Purpose is everywhere your passion lives.

What illuminates your heart?

The mention of its name flutters your spirit.

Take that passion and elevate. Study it, learn it, Do it for a living.

Your passion will change the World.You will step into a feeling of
never needing for nothing, for you will have everything you ever need.
Your life will exist in abundance.

Seek your truth first.

You have the power to define yourself.

Let your Definition of You Define your Legacy.

By C. Lynne Luster

Letter to my little Sista

If…

*I knew then what I know now I would tell my younger self,
she is worth more than what the average person thinks of
her. Why? Because she is EXTRAORDINARY. There is a
calling on your life to be more, see more and to do more. There
is nothing ordinary about you. The four walls you are surrounded
by, your block, your neighborhood, your friends and even your
family do not define you. You are EXTRAORDINARY and
only you can do what you were born to do. You have a special
place in the world and it is your job to learn, focus and work hard
for that place. Only YOU can fulfill your greatness because you
my dear beautiful, smart, strong, loving, intelligent, fabulous and
awesome young lady are EXTRAORDINARY.*

Your Sista,

Sinita Wells

Define what it means to be

EXTRAORDINARY to you:

_____

_____

_____

_____

_____

_____

_____

Hey Lil Sista,

Know your worth! You are so much more than doing things to fit in like following the crowd or wearing clothes showing your backside. Remember you are beautiful within you don't have to show your skin. Getting your education is the key to life not trying to catch a man just so you could be called wife. You have all the time in the world to have kids. So stay true to your dreams and desires in your life. When one door closes another door will open. Listen to your parents and sister stay focused, and the things that you do just make sure that they're worth it. It won't be easy but if you should fall you have a circle full of sisters who will help you through it all. We will never ever judge you. So... to my strong black sista be all you can be! Go to college and get your degree! Your bachelors, masters, and if you desire it, your PHD! And at the end of the day know you are worth it!

Love,

Shydra Berry

Know your Worth

Diamond in the rough- Someone (or something) that has hidden exceptional characteristics and/or future potential, but currently lacks the final touches that would make them truly stand out from the crowd.

A Letter to a Jewel in the making

Dearest Little Sista,

I hope that someone in your life has told you that you can be whatever you want to be. I actually prefer the Army's tagline "Be ALL you Can Be"; because I don't think we were created to be or do just one thing. Instead, I believe we were created to be many things to many people over many seasons in our lifetime.

I am not suggesting that you run out and try to do anything and everything that comes your way, but I think it is worse to be satisfied with achieving just one thing in life when you can do so much more!

At your age thinking about the future can be scary. Especially, if no one has ever told you that you could or would amount to anything in life. But, if no one has ever told you that you can rise above generational holds of teen pregnancy / drugs / miseducation / abuse

Tell the world "I Define Me"!

If you have never been told that you can excel at math; know that YOU can Crack the Code of Science and Technology Engineering and Math like Sister Kimberly Bryant of Black Girls Code.

If no one has told you that you are beautiful; know that YOU ARE because your skin tone, the texture of your hair, the shape of your lips, your height. The size of your frame were carefully selected by the Creator for a Divine purpose; and on the day that you were born He shouted to the other creatures in Heaven "Isn't She Lovely?"!!!!!

So if no one has ever told you that "you is kind, you is smart, you is important" allow me to be one of the first to tell you that no matter what mistakes you have made, you will RISE like author, actor, professor and writer Maya Angelou.

You may be thinking "you don't know me lady"; you don't know my struggles; and you are right. I don't know what neighborhood you come from. I don't know if your parents have money or if your family struggles each day to get by. Or, whether your family loves you unconditionally or if you have ever been the victim of any kind of abuse. I don't know if I am talking to a strong leader or a young lady who likes to hide in the background. So, how do I know that YOU WILL rise, ARE smart, ARE beautiful, WILL succeed?

Because when God created you, he sent you to earth with everything YOU need. You don't have what Halle Berry, Ashanti, China Anne McClain, Nicki Minja, or Beyonce have because you were meant for something different. The only thing missing is for you to figure out what that is and that takes time. You have to learn to listen in quiet moments to your own spirit because that is where the Almighty will connect with you. Even if you don't know the answers now, when someone tries to put you in a box that feels uncomfortable, send them away and proudly say I Define Me!

Your Big Sis,

N. Adewale

Little Sister,

I will not keep you long

I only have a few words that help me grow along

The evolutionary path that you are just beginning

First, you are already winning

You are your own competition, so only when you have tested
yourself do you rest

In all things, you are enough

You are pretty enough

You are intelligent enough

You have enough love

Your hair is good enough

Your butt/breasts/hips/ thighs are big enough

Little Sister,

I promise not to keep you long

I just want to tell you to never forget that song

The one that speaks to your heart

And reminds you of where to start

When you lose your center and get off track

Remember that what you give away, you cannot get back

Little Sister

You are a Queen

Your Queen-dom is within and not based on material things

Own your royalty

Leave a legacy

You are the finest

You are fabulous, Little Sister.

~Leia Ali

Define what it means when you hear the word ENOUGH

_____

_____

_____

_____

_____

_____

Statistics-Do they Define You???

*1 in 5 high school girls say they do not know three adults to whom to turn if they have a problem.

Let's redefine this statistic right now? List three women you know you can turn to:

1._____

2._____

3._____

In today's society our girls need to realize the importance of breaking cycles or allowing cycles to define you. The only way to be a cycle-breaker is to define the cycles and make a decision to say this will not be me. Awareness is the Key! So be aware! If you do not know what you stand for, society will define it for you!

You tell me? Is it true? Will these statistics define you? Or will you be a Keeper to self?

Cleansing My Soul-Stress 101

Let's talk about Stress baby...As if all of the changes happening in your body aren't enough, there are tons of outside pressures going on, too. You have school, homework, test, and maintaining good grades. You also might have a competitive sport that you practice every day. Plus, you have extracurricular activities to attend and then you have your friends and fun to think about. You also have pressure from your family ... there's also all of the stuff going on in the world that concerns you. It's enough to make a sista lose it! Oh and if you throw a relationship in the mix, help us all. I can see you feeling like help me.

Stress levels are always on 10! Your mom and dad don't understand, you are trying to define you and your friends are also out of control.

How do you handle this? Do you write, scream, shout or act out. Do you think of hurting yourself, shutting down or running away so that you don't go mad? First say to yourself, "this too shall pass" With a few tips I promise you, you can get through this. While stress isn't always a bad thing—a little bit might just push you to that extra step to make an A—too much can be overwhelming. In fact, too much stress can have negative effects on your health. Everyone handles stress differently, which means that what stresses you out could be just what your friend needs to be the best she can be so perhaps you can try this to reduce your stress level:

- **Identify the source:** Find out what has you down and make a conscious decision to let it go. Do not let problems take up space in your head rent free. SO free your mind by talking to your mom, sista, mentor or counselor!

- **Breathe:** Sometimes when you take a breather, it's easier to find a solution. I always say take a deep breath in and let go! Just remember to breathe out also! Breathe in and out!

- **Get healthy:** Nutrition can be a major factor when dealing with stress. Remember that saying, "You are what you eat"? Well, in a way, that's kind of true ... because what you put into your body determines how your body feels. Do you get it? Eat well, Be well!

- **Work it out:** Find a way to release tension, through exercise, Zumba, Nia NOW, yoga, walking or running. Working up a sweat and getting your heart rate going, will definitely make your body react positively. SO like Nike says "Just DO it!

- **Sleep:** Duh! You need it. No texting zone in your bed. Some of you need 8 hours, some less, but get it in! Sleep is crucial mentally, physically and spiritually. Sleep deprivation makes you irritable, and distracted. Not good! In order to get enough sleep, stay away from caffeine late in the day or before you plan to go to sleep; develop a regular sleep pattern (in other words, have a regular time you go to bed and get up); don't overdo the naps; make it easy to fall asleep by limiting noise and anything else that might distract you from sleeping; and learn your own sleeping habits.

- **Relax:** Wooosaah, Om! Namaste! Find what works for you and do it! Meditation works, music, journaling, being ok with being alone and not being alone is sooo necessary. Find the method that is right for you. Whatever it is that helps you reduce stress, do you!

Free Yo Mind! Stress Kit

Erasers, rubber bands, seeds, pennies, rocks or marbles, confetti, string, lip gloss

Erasers-make your mistakes disappear

Rubber Bands-help you stretch your limits

Mustard Seeds- have faith in your journey and remember you're always growing

A Penny- So you will never be broke

Marbles- don't lose your marbles

Confetti- to celebrate the joys in your life!

String- Keep it all together

Lip Gloss- Always Define your shine!

Chocolate- to always know life can be sweet

A Journal-to always write a new chapter

*Remember when God tells you to walk, Run like the Wind for you are guaranteed to fly!~DivineTea

Dating, sexual assault, and relationships

1.8 million of the 22.3 adolescents ages 12-17 in the U.S. have been victims of serious sexual assault.

*50% of the reported date rapes occur among teenagers. 1 in 5 teens who have been in a serious relationship report being hit, slapped or pushed by a partner.

*71% of teens regard boyfriends/girlfriends spreading rumors about them on cell phones and social networking sites as a serious problem.

*1 in 4 teens in a relationship (25%) says they have been called names, harassed, or put down by their partner through cell phones and texting.   *68% of teens say boyfriends/girlfriends sharing private or embarrassing pictures/videos on cell phones and computers are a serious problem.

*1 in 3 teens (30%) say they are text messaged 10, 20, 30 times an hour by a partner inquiring where they are, what they're doing, or who they're with.

*1 in 2 teens who have been in serious relationships state they've gone against their beliefs in order to please their partner.

*1 in 4 teens who have been in a serious relationship say their boyfriend or girlfriend has tried to prevent them from spending time with friends or family; the same number have been pressured to only spend time with their partner.

*1 in 3 girls between the ages of 16 and 18 say sex is expected for people their age if they're in a relationship; half of teen girls who have experienced sexual pressure report they are afraid the relationship would break up if they did not give in.

*Nearly 1 in 4 girls who have been in a relationship (23%) reported going further sexually than they wanted as a result of force or pressure.

What is body image?

Body image is the reflection you see when you look in the mirror. Is it complicated? Yes, so let me break it down for you.

Body image is how you perceive your physical appearance, and how you feel about your body, particularly your weight and figure. Body image is the feeling you get when you start to look at other girls and compare yourself. Especially when you begin to feel uncomfortable in your jeans or bathing suits. How it feels when you go to the mall and you feel nothing looks good on you at all. This can cause excessive stress, anxiety and frustration. Lots of girls are constantly told to be happy the way you are but it is difficult when society is promoting messages that being "overweight" is unattractive when at the end of the day, every girl is different and there are all types of body weights. Remember genetics has alot to do with it, know that every girl will not be a model size so we shouldn't try to defy the odds, we want to be happy, we want to look in the mirror daily and say thank you God for the body you gave me.

I usta hate my lips, my hair, small breast and thought I was waay to skinny. I wanted to look like my mom, she had hips and thighs. As an African-American she was considered a ten, 36-24-36, what some would call a brickhouse. So for me it was a constant challenge, because after all I had to learn to define me. You may feel the opposite, feeling you're too thick, breast to big, hair too curly or too straight. Are we ever 100% happy? Of course not.

One way to develop a healthy and realistic body image is to pay less attention to what you see on videos, TV, commercials and music that gives you a masculine point of view. You might also find out about different cultures where the "in" look may be a lot different than what we're told is ideal here in your neighborhood. So focusing on what you like about your body and appearance is an important step in feeling better about yourself.

Do you love the natural curl pattern in your hair? Your almond eyes, pretty smile, long neck or cute toes? It is important to define the things you love and can learn to appreciate, and pay less attention to the parts of your body that will be constantly changing in your lives.

The more physically active girls are, the greater their self-esteem and the more satisfied they are with their weight, regardless of how much they weigh. Confidence starts within, and it isn't defined in a dress size so wear yours on the outside!

Body Image Statistics

*92% of teen girls would like to change something about the way they look, with body weight ranking the highest.

*75% of teenage girls felt 'depressed, guilty and shameful after spending just three minutes leafing through a fashion magazine.

*70% of girls ages 15 to 17 avoid normal daily activities such as attending school, going to the doctor, or even giving their opinion "due to feeling badly about one's looks."

*61% of all women and 69 % of girls (15 to 17) feel that their mother has had a positive influence on their feelings about themselves and their beauty.

*90% of eating disorders are found in girls

*Yet 40% of girls' ages 11-17 say they do not play sports because they do not feel skilled or competent and 23% do not think their bodies look good.

*Girls' view physical and emotional health as closely connected. For example, more than 1/3 of girls ages 11–17 reported eating more when they are "stressed out" and overweight girls are more than twice as likely as girls who are not overweight to report eating more in times of stress.

More than 60% of teenage girls skip breakfast at least once a week and nearly 20% skip it every day.

Social Peer Pressures, Media and Marketing

The media, including television, movies, videos, song lyrics, magazines, the internet, video games and advertisements, all too often portray girls and women in a sexual manner—revealing clothing, body posture and facial expressions. These images become the models of femininity that girls—from a very early age—learn to emulate. Girls are constantly barraged by this message: Women in our society are valued above all else based on their physical attractiveness.

The sexualization of girls in all forms of media is a "broad and increasing problem and is harmful to girls' self-image and healthy development," according to a 2007 report by the American Psychological Association Task Force. Sexualization is defined as occurring when a person's value comes only from her or his sexual appeal or behavior, to the exclusion of other characteristics, and when a person is sexually objectified, e.g., made into a thing for another's sexual use.

*74% of girls say they are under pressure to please everyone

44

*3 out of 4 girls say they feel pressure to be "super girls"

*74% say they often feel stressed

*Teenagers between the ages of 12 and 14 who use media with high sexual content are up to 2.2 times more likely to have sex by the time they are 16 than those who use less such media.

*1 in 5 high school girls say they do not know three adults to whom to turn if they have a problem.

Self-esteem

Low self-esteem is a thinking disorder in which an individual views him/herself as inadequate, unlovable, and/or incompetent. Once formed, this negative view permeates every thought, producing faulty assumptions and ongoing self-defeating behavior.

A new, long-term study of self-esteem in adolescents and young adults shows that race and body mass are important predictors of self-esteem in adolescent women. Self-worth is greater in black women after age 11 and that self-esteem is lower in both black and white women with the highest body mass indexes. "However, building self-esteem could improve outcomes, as suggested by a community-based study that notes lower rates of violent behaviors in those who underwent self-esteem building."

*Over 70% of girls age 15 to 17 avoid normal daily activities, such as a 75% of girls with low self-esteem reported engaging in negative activities like cutting, bullying, smoking, drinking, or disordered eating. This compares to 25% of girls with high self-esteem.

Sexual harassment, Alcohol and drug influences

Past research has shown that girls involved with sports in high school are less likely to engage in risky sexual behaviors such as high numbers of partners, inconsistent or no use of birth control, or engaging in sex while under the influence of drugs or alcohol. The decrease in girls' participation in risky sexual behavior associated with sports involvement is partly due to a delay in sexual initiation and partly to social-psychological dynamics, such as enhanced self-confidence, a less stereotypically feminine gender role identity, and/or a stronger desire to avoid teenage pregnancy.

*Around 30% of teens said their first sexual experience occurred during school hours or between the hours of 3 p.m. and 5 p.m. Most have sex in their home or at a friend's house.

*3 in 10 girls become pregnant as a teen, more than half of U.S. teens ages 15-17 have had oral sex, with 70% of those ages 18-19 having had oral sex. Only 9% reported using a condom during oral sex.

Half of all new HIV infections in the United States still occur in people who are under 25-years-old and teenagers who take "virginity pledges" are almost as likely to be infected with a sexually transmitted disease as those who never made the pledge.

Some teens (3.5% out of 13,000--boys and girls) also say they have exchanged sex for money or drugs

3 million teens become infected with one or more STDs each year.

*279 teenage girls between the ages of 14 and 17 were interviewed about their relationships and sex.

*Know your Body, Know your Status, and never have unprotected sex. Never, ever, ever!

41% said that, on at least one occasion, they had sex when they didn't want to. *10% said that their boyfriends forced them to have sex. 38% of those girls also admitted to having unwanted sex because they were afraid that their boyfriend would be angry if they said no. *8 out of 10 female teenagers had a partner who was at least one year older than they were at first sexual intercourse (81%), compared with just under one-half of males (46%).

*1 in 6 teenagers aged 15-17 has not engaged in sexual intercourse, but has given or received oral sex, and very few of these teenagers have used a condom.

*Minority teens have been particularly hard hit by HIV/AIDS: Teen girls account for 58% of new AIDS cases reported among young people ages 13-19. * African American and Latino teens account for most of new AIDS cases among teens at 60% and 24% respectively.

*8 out of 10 students say they have experience some form of sexual harassment at school.

*Girls are harassed more often than boys with 83% saying they have endured sexual comments—including homophobic remarks—teasing, touching or rumors.

 *If you choose to have sex, make a pledge to yourself that regardless of your relationship status, you are accountable for your body so make sure you and your partner get tested.

Cyber-bullying

- 1 in **10** young people are victims of cyber bullying

- **37%** of them are experiencing cyber bullying on a highly frequent basis

- **20%** of young people are experiencing extreme cyber bullying on a daily basis

- New research suggests that young males and females are equally at risk of cyber bullying

- Young people found to be twice as likely to be cyber bullied on Facebook as on any other social network. Red Flag?

- **54%** of young people using Facebook reported that they have experienced cyber bullying on the social network

- Facebook, Ask.FM and Twitter found to be the most likely sources of cyber bullying, being the highest in traffic of all social networks.

- Cyber bullying found to have catastrophic effects upon the self-esteem and social lives of up to **70%** of young people

Social change

*Only 1 in 3 teens polled (33%) believe that knowledge is a key to success

*74% think college is necessary to meet their career goals.

*More than 57% of all respondents say their children will have more challenges than they have.

*When asked "What things can make life better for future generations?" almost 40% said finishing school.

22% said being involved in their communities. 13% said pushing for equal opportunities for everyone.

*When we spoke to girls in our SistaKeeper Circles 90% stated role models, mentors and positive messages from women whom have walked a similar path they feel can help break down barriers and break cycles because it allows them to define their personal vision and see positive solutions.

#I Define Me!!!

Who defines Me? Well, Click on my facebook status and you will see look at me now! Yet, now doesn't mean forever because you see my life is complicated, can't post everything because my family is watching. Perhaps I will get a like or a comment , or maybe I will slide on over to glide to get my video on, don't ask FM about me, just wait for set out Sunday and you will see, all of a sudden I am instagram famous because I got caught up with my (MCM) Male Crush Monday. All at the click of a button. I wasn't thinking, just textin my feelings.

You tell me? Was it worth it? Your reputation and all the gossip, the undercover life you living. Who got time for that? When you failing geometry and chemistry. Yet you got time to snapchat, kik back and turnup on Tuesday and you say you are not a cell phone junkie.

You say you are not addicted, then put the phone down and listen for a minute. Social media can be beautiful if you use it to make a difference, not being a statistic, spending time taking selfies, instead of self-reflecting. While you're thinking, how about stop sneak dissing on your sista and google cyber-bullying. Know that hurt people, hurt people, now repeat it and if you think you might forget it then re-tweet it. Quit trying to be a mean girl, co-starring in your own pretty little liar reality show. Don't you know it's Tell-Lie-Vision. The social media game will keep changing, so it is up to you to define your mission today, do not allow your digital footprint be your history, when next week you will be trying to delete it. IJS…

SO… you tell me, you say you will not allow social media to define you, if so then what will your #hashtag be? As for me, my brand speaks so the world can see it, if you want to know, follow me. #IdefineMe

By DivineTea

50

Dear Lil Sista,

You have heard it all, "Girl, you have baby making hips," and "Y'all need to watch her. "All that behind; she probably doing something." Perhaps, the female adults in your life insulted you about your physique and judged your sexuality because of the way you were built up. You have been ridiculed, lips have been smacked, eyes have been rolled, and the men have whistled. Grown men have admired you and women who were supposed to teach you instead rolled their eyes in disgust.

All the boys in school did whatever they could to get a 'feel' while the girls have made you feel as if something is wrong with you. In elementary school, you refused to join the Jr. Cheerleaders because you didn't want your skirt to ride too high in the back.

In middle school, you wore a jacket to hide your body from the entire school. You have wondered how you can just fit in. How can you look like everyone else and be accepted by the people who you so desperately want to place their stamp of approval on you? You spent all of your teen years hating to be cursed with such a big butt. I am writing this letter to you thirty years later because I want you to know that the body you have is the body God gave you. No matter what other people think, your responsibility is to show your body love by embracing the skin you are in, eating healthily and wholly, and to treating your body with all the respect and kindness it deserves.

Here's when you know a young lady values the body God gave her and the relationship that He longs to have with her.

She finds something she loves to do that honors God and she does it, without being asked or cajoled. She won't allow negative influences to distract her. Even if that negative influence is a poor diet, an improper use of her body, or friends who want her to participate in alcohol and or drugs, she will find quiet time to meet with God and hear what he wants from her.

Lil' Sista, there is no denying that where you are in life right now is a difficult space. When I was in high school, I constantly looked at my peers and thought, "Wow, I wish I had designer clothes, purses, and shoes like hers," or "If I could get that kind of haircut, more boys would like me." Silly me, I was trying to define who I was by looking at others. It took me all these years to know and understand it is not the clothes on my body, the way I wear my hair, the car I drive, or the size of my butt that define me.

The fact that I am patient, kind, content, hardworking, faithful, well-versed, well rounded, and intelligent determines who I am. My gift to the world is that I listen to God and He directs me with the words I type and the actions I take.

To conclude this letter, I want to issue you a challenge. I believe you honor God when you show your body love, embrace the skin you are in, eat healthily and wholly, and find an activity that you can do every day that honors your temple. Will you take the next 30 days to demonstrate to everyone around you that you are committed to walking in your gift by saying no to anything that distracts you?

Say this aloud,
I am the Keeper of my body.
I am the Keeper of my food choices.
I am the Keeper of my physical activities.
I am the Keeper of me.

Please take my advice,
Your Big Sis!
Kem Smith

I am the **Keeper** of…..

_____

_____

_____

_____

_____

_____

_____

_____

_____

_____

Heart Beats

My heart beats for you, for that sista that is seeking the meaning of love, for that sista who dares to look in the mirror & feel your soul! My heart beats for you, lil sista who lost your virginity at 12 or 13 years old, teen pregnancy became your reality, or low self-esteem has become your last name, never loving self because friends called you too dark, too light, too tall, too short, too skinny, too fat, labeling you straight or gay, instead of your name. What a shame!

My heart, your story is very similar to mine. I was the baby inside the belly of a teen mom. People told her she would be nothing, she should give up on her dreams, but instead she birthed me. My heart beats for that sista who loves to fight to protect herself from the streets, she says momma chose Tom, Dick n Harry over me, so you now choose to love a brother who grew up with no mother. So he treats you like eye candy, and you eat it up, you swallow the bitter with the sweet, while HIV and STD's become your possibilities instead of high school graduations and universities! My sista I want you to reclaim your identity.

Whether you were molested, or having a baby or dealing with a lifetime of one mistake that has given you a label, know that God knows your heart, and on any given night he will restore your thoughts. Sure suicide, homelessness, foster care and family dysfunction may be your start, but know God will cover you and be your protection. God is waiting to be your salvation. We all need a solid foundation but know the relationship with God is all about you and your heart.

My heart beats for you my sista, and I ask of you not to give up. My teen mom gave me all she got. While statistics counted us out, but look at me now! Now is the time to define your tomorrow!

I thank God he had our back and he listened to the beat of our hearts. So if you feel you got nothing, know Jesus is always waiting to step in your spot. He will lead you from emptiness to success and it won't cost you a dime because your trials and tribulations are paid for in his blood.

My heartbeats for you and I pray you make it through this life lesson. I believe in you, but you must believe in yourself, know you too can beat this! But you must listen to your heart!

DivineTea

54

Create your own playlist of music that defines the BEATS
that play in your HEART! Now listen to it in solitude!

_____
_____
_____
_____
_____
_____
_____
_____
_____

My dearest little sister,

Can I bend your ear for a minute to speak to the essence of you?
I want to be a shoulder for your burdens, and for your tears, a tissue.
As your eyes soak in these words know that you are beautiful
Your inner and outer presence makes you an individual
Life may throw you many curveballs some you may catch and some
may fall. Focus more on how things feel when they happen and less on
if you drop the ball. Let your spirit guide you in every decision and
learn a lesson from everything you go through

Please don't get so caught up in a man that you forget to consider you
Somebody is going to break your heart in life, It's gonna happen a time
or two
Shed your tears, scream, and holla but also snap back and regroup
Please don't allow your pain to punish others, forgive them and
yourself too!
Understand that those who cause pain are also victims of their own
issues. If you feel like giving up on life, sit in the feeling and process
the root
Close your eyes and connect to your spirit as it is the God in you.
Respect your body, feelings, and thoughts at all times, they are yours
and nobody else's
Everything that is a part of you is a compilation of your essence.
If there comes a time when you are unhappy with the way you are
viewed
Realize your issue, admit it to yourself, create a plan to work and
reinvent you
Surround yourself with positivity and people doing things inspiring and
new. Try not to find yourself being the only light in every room you
walk into.
It's ok not to know everything, learning from your mistakes is the
greatest blessing
If you wake up the next day to try again, dust your shoulders off and
embrace the lesson.

My dearest little sister, lastly, there will be those who try to break you
Pay attention to the actions of others and remember that YOU are the
only one that defines YOU!

Peace, Love, Empowerment, and Growth.
Forever your Big Sister,
Candice E. Cox

God's Queen

A woman. Who can find her? For her price is far above rubies.

In her effortless commitment to fulfill the Lord Duties, She constantly seeks after the Lord, Asking, "What must I do?" Understanding that without Christ she is a woman without a clue; she is up late pacing the floors of her home, praying and crying for her family, being fully persuaded in Christ.

A woman.

Who can find her?

She waits.

She prays.

She seeks.

She listens.

She is a woman who was lost but surely is found in Christ.

Engulfed in his Will; Submerged in his Presence. She is the beautiful fragrance of incense; her aura of holiness consumes the room. She is an atmosphere setter, she is the perfect verse of a romantic love letter.

She loves - oh her love - The strength and the courage that exudes from her very heart and seeps through her pores.

This woman her cup runs over.

She is illuminating; she is holy.

This woman, she is amazing. She is God's Queen. Some may often wonder, but God's light - it speaks when she steps onto the scene. Her words aren't mean, but rather kind and wise. Oh when she speaks her eloquent speech corrects and convicts in love.

A woman.

Who can find her? The search isn't difficult, but we - yes we - sometimes forget our God identity when the identity of this world consumes our heart our minds and yes our spirits.

A woman.

Who can find her? Is it you Queen? Yes, queen. Ladies I speak of each and every one of you - God's Queen.

Have you found her? Have you even said hi to her? Or have you been too busy to find to even acknowledge her? I assure you she isn't far; she dwells in the heart of Christ; she gleams in his glory; she sits at his feet; she diligently seeks his face. Who can find her? Where is she? Am I too late?

No not at all Queens you are indeed on time. This very day you are on time. I've been waiting for you God says, "I see you took time to find you when all the while I knew you. I called you special before you were born; you were mine before the foundation. "You are mine!"

"Allow me to reintroduce myself, my Queen." "I Am the… I Am that I Am!" "I am your God, Queen; make it personal"

"I am your King!" "I am your Lord!" "You belong to me my Queen!"

A woman.

 Who can find her? For her prices is far above rubies. God's Queen, you are special and you are priceless. You are the Proverbs 31 woman. Say hello today to the Queen in you.

Hello……Written By: Christian Cooper

Little Sista

I am looking in the mirror but I don't like what I see, I know deep inside that it
is time to change feelings that I feel about me but you see, It all began with a
stare, I don't like the stares and I don't like the feeling the stares give me...
I feel like I am giving off some type of aura, like hey look at me, because I am
getting back a form of expression that is so unclear to me.
I wish I would have learned the lesson in dressing so naïve, skirts above my
knees, shirts, revealing my stomach, no bra and all, but I was just expressing
me, a young girl, just fourteen, But the stares I received were warm, but
intimidating, I was having intimate sessions with strangers on a daily basis, and
no one really knew the inner me.
So I am looking in this mirror, wondering what's in this obsession, I must
escape the desires that have taken over my temple of youth, my innocence was
stolen as I stand swayin my hips to the beat, saying hey look at me, but don't
touch, but don't I look good, I feel good too, and you like looking at me don't
you and I guess you like it too, but do you have to stare so deep, deep into my
insides. I'm just a baby, perpetrating twenty, trying to get my groove on.
While you trying to give me pennies for my thoughts; stealing away my mind,
while violating my emotions, my physical, my spirit, my temple, my time.
Now, here I am left feeling loss, paying the cost, because you didn't seem to
see my innocence, my pureness, you snatched my virginity like a thief in the
night, squeezing me uncontrollably, holding me, exposing me. You were only
suppose to look and admire from afar, but you got in to my space and took over
my privacy, leaving me with nothing, emptiness, and unconsciousness.

I did not ask for this, this is not bliss, this is the risk I took by allowing you to look at me, but you didn't have to take me, couldn't you have just looked at my inner beauty, just taking a peak, not force yourself inside of me, but you couldn't stand the heat, you had to have me, you took me without me saying yes....No, I did not feel blessed, because I did not ask for this. Look at me I'm such a mess, didn't you know I was a virgin, only fourteen, couldn't you read in between the lines, my skin, my voice, my body shouted: I am too young for this!!! Sure I smiled, while you stared at me, but you didn't see what I was trying to say, I didn't want a baby, I just wanted someone to notice me, I just wanted someone to notice me. Making this princess feel like a queen.

What is it in the lesson society has taught me, that my inner spirit does not validate me? Am I not a queen, don't I have meaning....

For so long I looked in that mirror, feeling ashamed of the beauty God has given me. Trying to search deep inside to find the true me because you see all I longed for was a little attention, all I wanted was for someone to love me unconditionally....

So now I thank GOD for my spiritual healing... I know I am a queen and I say to all my sisters of the universe that it's time for us to take back our earth, it's time for a rebirth... nurture your soul, nurture your spirit, nurture your essence, meditate and think first, but remember before healing others you must learn to love thyself first. Heal thyself and love thyself first... love thyself first.

Little Sista.

DivineTea

60

Little Sista,

This letter reaches out to all of my little sisters. I may not be your biological sister but I am your sista and I wish you the best. I pray that you learn and grasp this thing called life much quicker than I.

First and foremost God does not make mistakes. God is all-knowing and perfect in every way. From the crown of your head, to your feet that are planted firmly to the ground God has created you as a mighty vessel, a vessel that holds a strong, bold and powerful spirit.

You must know that there may be times when insecurity and doubt of your abilities might show up. Fear may take a hold and cause doubt to creep in. But don't allow it to paralyze you. Believe that you are great because you are!

Grow into a woman with principles. Know that sometimes you will have to stand up for what you believe in. Know that sometimes you will have to speak your mind and that you may have to face the uncomfortable task of placing people where they belong. However, always execute it with tactfulness and fairness, but don't shy away when speaking your mind.

Literally learn to look in the mirror at your beautiful self. Embrace your lovely tresses, your skin tone and the body you were blessed with.

Learn to not only love, but to forgive those that have hurt you. Leave negativity at the door and remove yourself from it if at all possible.

Remember that no one wants to be around a Bitter Betty, so don't forget to smile. Never tolerate mess or settle for less. You're worth more than that.

My sista don't allow others to write your life story. You are your own author. Only you can define you. Do these things because life is a journey that will not last forever...

Written By: Eleanie Campbell

I define me as **ROYALTY** because

_____
_____
_____
_____
_____
_____
_____
_____
_____

Remember…Being Royalty doesn't mean you place yourself on a pedestal!

Education the Key to My Destiny

I keep telling myself I ain't worth it. They keep telling me to go to school, but me and school ain't jiving. I ain't got time for this nonsense. I could be doing something else. Ain't nobody in my family finish school. So why they think school gone work for me. Ain't nobody graduate. Ain't nobody got a job. And when I share my dreams and aspirations they laugh at me. They tell me I'm a fool. I ain't nothing, I ain't gone be nothing, so I might as well quit. I tell myself forget them; you can be what you want to be. While they laugh at me I keep pushing. While they make fun of me I grind harder. I hold the key to my destiny, and my destiny tells me I am phenomenal that's me. I am Sojourner, I am Harriet, I am Fannie Lou, I am Mary McLeod Bethune. I am Marva Collins. I am every woman that does what is necessary to speak, live and walk the truth. So while they keep laughing at me I'm a hold my head high apply myself and appreciate my worth. School is cool, I'm no fool. I'm destined to be the best I can be.

Just wait and you will see.

Sure sometimes life throws you a curve ball. Whether you were born into wealth and due to your parents work schedule you rarely see them, or you were born into the circumstance of poverty and your family struggles each day to get by; education is the key to your destiny. I just want you to know I love you. As a matter of fact I am crazy in love with you. Please know that everything about you is outstanding. The way you walk, talk and strut your stuff. You are a heavenly angel. You are god's gift to the world; simply because you were born a girl. Now how cool is that. Girl you know you ROCK! Now take a minute

63

and think about how you shine bright like a diamond and shower the world with your talents and abilities. Do you know what you have to offer the world? The answer is staring you right in the face. It is something you partake in five days a week, nine months out of the year. Come on it is on the tip of your tongue. Alright, alright, alright it's going to school. **"The Essence of Education"** requires that you nurture your mind, body and soul. In order to do that you must fully embrace the opportunities your education presents you each and every day. Each and every day as a result of going to school you position yourself to do great and marvelous things. You position yourself to live the life you were meant to live. By going to school you expose yourself to various cultures, different mindsets, values, critical thinking and power. You separate yourself from the masses as you know education is the greatest gift one could ever give and receive.

Education is paramount as it creates a level playing field for everyone. Once you have it no one can take it from you. It is yours to have, yours to honor, yours to respect and yours to protect. It and it alone allows a blind man to see, a deaf man to hear, and a mute man to speak. Education is a natural high. It will have you floating singing a new song unto the lord because it opens your eyes to the challenges, obstacles, joys and pains of the world we live in. It gives you room to think for yourself and to make decisions based on sound evidence. You are not only able to talk about what you read about or heard about. You are able to talk from a lived experience. It is one thing to see it on television. It is another thing to read about it in a book, however; to be able to discuss your experience is priceless.

Do not let anyone one tell you that an education does not matter. An education is not important. Believe me when I say they are lying to you. They are attempting to set you up for failure. Don't fall for the okie- doke. Smile and just let them talk, and when they finish tell them that is interesting. The numbers don't lie. Research shows that the more education you have the quality of life you live is better. Whether you talk about job satisfaction, health, personal earnings, or unemployment college graduates outperform peers with less education (Pew Research, 2014). It is that simple. Having an education pays off in the long run. So at the end of the day going to school is really cool, as you are rewarded a quality life.

A quality life and notice I keep using the word quality. Dictionary.com defines quality as an essential or distinctive characteristic, character with respect to fineness or grade of excellence, a personality or character trait. A quality life means you are living and walking in excellence. You not only know, but understand your value and what it is you bring to the table. You except and expect nothing but the best because anything less is unacceptable. You appreciate what life has to offer and are grateful that your allegiance to education opened your eyes. Baby girl education is the key to your destiny. It will afford you opportunities of a life time. You will be able to go where you never thought you would go. You will be able to do what you never thought you could do. You will be true to yourself by living, loving and enjoying life. You will not apologize for being who you are and you will not allow others to disrespect, dehumanize, or downplay your capabilities because you are a girl.

You are a girl and it is an honor and privilege to be in your presence. Your spirit radiates happiness. Your smile exalts sunshine. Your tears are puddles of distinction. You are God's immeasurable gift. It is time for you to spread your wings and fly. You will blossom into a beautiful rose. Its beauty is in the eye of the beholder, its fragrance heightens senses, and its strength withstands the test of time. You are a girl a mighty blessing to the world.

Written By: Shonta Smith

I define my Essence of **EDUCATION** by reaching my essence of development by accomplishing my number one goal:

_____

_____

_____

Pretty Girl Swag

If it is all about you, why do you allow her to break you down, turn your smile into a frown. Allow young men with no boundaries to control your mind? Why do we second guess ourselves when we know better!

He says you are pretty, beautiful, your body is a ten, its banging, yet when you look in the mirror you can't see it, but you believe him; when you know he has a plan. Do you love you? Lil Sista, I ask you, do you love you?

Our young men walk around showing their backsides; while some girls advertise their breast and thighs like they are a number two, telling society to have it your way, like a side order at Burger King. When do you say no way!

When are you gonna feed your mind, body and spirit, and say I'm a full meal deal, with some eat fresh substance. Define where is God in your life and say no to the okie-doke! Facebook photos displaying bathroom poses, in a private space displaying public photos, allowing pretty to be defined by your stomach and lips, when you realize that being the average girl in a video, is not you! Your more than your hips! Your mind is pretty and you my sista are beautiful!

Sisters please realize beauty starts on the inside. Respect starts at home, yet we act like momma is old. She don't know, she was your age 20 years ago, but see she didn't have cell phones and skype video, she don't shorthand text, that was used in college notes, she wrote love letters, she is ole' school. Yet she constantly says watch how you walk, the words that flow out your mouth and how you look when you walk out the house and how you respond when u get talked about, get your education and wait for the babies! Smile at your haters and say later to the bad boys with no goals or positive occupations.

Sista, let the world know I'm not afraid to represent me. Just know that it takes a leader to stand alone and be the change you want to see. Know your history from the words of Ghandi, to Dr, Maya Angelou, Rise today. Why not now? Look in the mirror, you know the ending...as Micheal Jackson puts it. It is all about you, so make that change! Let the world see your Pretty Girl Swag, just make sure you know the words, make sure if it's all about you...it shows from the way u speak, the way you represent, the clothes you wear and the company you keep! You are a beautiful flower! And this is your time to shine, yes you are a Keeper, but you gotta believe it to achieve that pretty girl swag!

DivineTea

A Lesson on forgiveness~

Forgiveness After the Fact....

Ladies, know that when you hold grudges and do not forgive others you are simply hurting self because healing starts from within. No matter who has hurt you, God will help you heal through that hurt because he wants you to be the best you can be!! I learned at a later stage in my life how heavy un-forgiveness can weigh on you. Losing my mother at the age of 16 started a battle of chaos that I could have easily avoided... if only I just forgave.

Growing up my mother was not around because she had an itch. An itch of substance use that she could not shake and more than likely was not ready to shake because she hadn't been through enough 'changes' yet. Regardless I grew a huge button of hatred towards her. I would not call her mother. I would not talk to her and if I did I was rude. Even when being corrected by adults I still defied her. I would call my grandmother and aunties 'mother' in front of her to hurt her feelings, but it never worked.

She knew I would come around.

She just did not know that it would come after she left this earth.

Even when I talked to her for the last time I was really rude. She called me three days before my 16th birthday and I think she knew something was going to happen. Her words were 'If I don't talk to you before your Birthday, Happy Birthday Baby momma loves you'. I was soooo hung up on this call happening on a day that was not my birthday; sure as she said I did not talk to her on my birthday, matter of fact I never heard her voice again.

My family told me time and time again that I needed to stop holding a grudge towards my mother, that she had a sickness.... I felt that it was blah blah blah blah blah but the moment I heard the words 'your mother has died' I immediately wished that I had let go of the grudges. I went through grief in a different way, I just didn't think about my mother or the pain that was brewing inside of me. I went three years without dealing with my mother's death and this is when forgiveness came. I had to work on forgiving myself for the continued hatred I expressed towards her. It took time and now I am at a place where I can think of her and not feel bad but can sit and remember the good times that we did have, like when we would play dress up and I would wear her heels and pearls around the house. When we would make peanut butter sandwiches then drink ice-cold milk. We always had fun together when I was young and could not completely comprehend what my mother was going through.

I also forgave my mother for her absence in my life, once I understood the illness that she was battling with I felt nothing but love for her. She went through a lot and while I may not agree with how she dealt with her illness she did the best that she knew how to do. It took her dying for me to figure out and understand, I now cherish her, and some could say well why now?

I completely can relate to the saying, you cannot help what you were born into, mental illness runs through my family and I know I could possibly have some in the future if I do not continue to take care of myself. Everything I do, I do in the honor of my mother who was a great mother and woman who simply did not know her own strength.

Written By: Javania M. Webb

In memory of Marilyn V. Webb

Forgiveness starts with me...I forgive myself for

_____

_____

_____

_____

_____

_____

_____

_____

_____

_____

Never Let Anyone Stop You from being Amazing!!!

As a freshman sitting on the steps at my high school my heart was so heavy watching all the other girls trying out for the freshman soccer team. My confidence in myself was at the lowest point it had ever been. The problem had started when I started to hear other students some which happen to be my very own friends say "black girls do not play soccer" "soccer is a white girl sport ".

Those very words spoke loud into my spirit and instantly created doubt in myself like I had never experienced before. It created a conflict within in myself to choose if I wanted to defy the odds and go down on the field and show them that black girls can play soccer because I was one of them and could actually play very well, or give up on the only sport that I had played since I was 3 years old and absolutely loved. My stomach felt like it was in my shoes as I continued to watch my chance at making the soccer team fade away as the tryouts continued to go on without me.

Until all of a sudden I developed this feeling inside me that I would like to now describe as courage take over. I pulled my cell phone out of my book bag and decided to call my mother for some much need advice. Just hearing her voice instantly soothed my soul.

 I remember telling her all about how I had been crying because I was so afraid of what everyone would say about me playing soccer and not being able to fit in because I played a sport that was not too familiar by others. I can also remember her exact words in telling me that "People are going to talk about you no matter if you're doing good or bad things that's just life baby so you might as well give them something good!!"

She then added how great of a soccer player I was and that if I tried out she would bet her last dollar that I would not only make the team but would be the star player!! You know that moms always have a way to make things better and it worked.

I immediately ran to the locker room to put my soccer things on and ran back as fast as I could down to the tryouts.

I approached the coach and told him how I was afraid to follow my heart and tryout because of what others would say and admitted that I was being very foolish in my thinking. He made me feel so much better by welcoming me out to tryout and added that he had been watching me sitting on the top of the hill and was waiting patiently for me to finally make up in my mind to come down.

The coach had already heard that I was a good soccer player from the junior high coaches and was already very excited at the possibility of my addition to the team. He noticed when tryouts began that he didn't see me out on the field but instead he saw me sitting up at the top of the hill. He had already assumed I had a personal dilemma I had to sort through but knew after I had it figured out the rest would be history.

So imagine that I had more people rooting for me to succeed than the few individuals that helped in creating the initial doubt. I ended up trying out the 3days of tryouts and secured a starting position on the freshman team and a week later asked to move up to the junior varsity team. Look at God so what God has for you is for you.

Never be afraid or discouraged to reach your dreams.

You define you and your legacy is your story you create so make it a great one. It all starts with you!!

Never Let Anyone Stop You from being Amazing!!!

Written By: Rhonika Jones

Define your Amazing:

_____

_____

_____

_____

_____

_____

_____

_____

_____

_____

_____

_____

_____

_____

Dear Perfectly Imperfect,

Being a teenager can be the most difficult time of your life trust me, it wasn't that long ago for me. But what I do wish is that I had my current self, be able to tell my past self a few things. I thought I might share those things with you.

1) Life is tough. That is a fact but trust me when I say, that *you* are tougher.

2) In a world that's constantly trying to change you, the best thing you can do is stay true to yourself. Peer pressure does exist but even more than your peers, are strangers. Don't let them break you because like I said in number one, you are tougher.

3) I'm sure you've heard that sticks and stones can break your bones but words can never hurt you, right? Well it's a lie. It's true that sticks and stones can indeed break your bones but bones heal. People will never forget how you made them feel with your words. They do the most damage because what's heard cannot be unheard.

4) I'm sure you own a mirror and probably a television. I'm even sure that you've compared yourself to a couple of celebrities. You are beautiful in your own way. Key word being: **Your**. You weren't meant to look like anybody else. Do me a favor? Every time you look in the mirror, compliment yourself. Love starts from within. So love yourself first and watch others fall in line.

5) Knowledge is **power**. I bet you're wondering why I bolded those words huh? Well it's simple, my Mother told me a long time ago that looks will fade but my intelligence will blossom. To learn is to grow. Never hit a plateau. Never hit your peak. Keep growing.

6) Lastly, I want you to know that you have purpose. God put you here for a reason. You may not realize what your purpose is yet but trust me. You have one. You are special. You are amazing. You are exactly what God wanted you to be.

I don't have all the answers. Trust me, I'm not the wisest out there but I do have a past and I'm sure you do too. Don't let your past define you. You define you. You make your own destiny. You control your future. There is a cheat to life: always enjoy it being you.

"Love yourself. Forgive yourself. Be true to yourself. How you treat yourself sets the standard for how others will treat you." — Steve Maraboli

Love,

Your Older Sista Lexi

Dear Beautiful Divine Sista,

How have you been? Have you been kind-hearted and gentle with yourself? Try not to worry about all that drama that happened yesterday. It doesn't matter today. Did you learn from it? Grow from it? Become better because of it? Then beloved, that's all you can expect from yourself. I remember when you would get so angry because you felt betrayed by a supposedly good friend. Remember how your heart ached? Remember how you said bad things about that person because they hurt you? Sweetie, I will tell you that forgiving others for hurting you is part of God's Divine plan for us. You are going to marvel at what happens to you, through you and for you because you opened your heart and chose forgiveness rather than revenge. You may not know what these words mean right now, but you will.....

"I hope you never lose your sense of wonder
You get your fill to eat but always keep that
hunger
May you never take one single breath for
granted
God forbid love ever leave you empty handed
I hope you still feel small when you stand beside
the ocean
Whenever one door closes I hope one more
opens
Promise me that you'll give faith a fighting
chance
And when you get the choice to sit it out or
dance'"

I Hope You Dance!!!!!

With Love,

By: Michelle Elgin

You Are More Than Enough

By Marie Chewe-Elliott

My precious sista:

Embrace this phase of your life and know that you –just as you are today – are enough. "Enough?" you may ask. Yes, enough! You are smart **enough**, good **enough**, beautiful **enough** to become your best version of you and all you are meant to be. It is important that you find a way of conveying and reaffirming this message to yourself every day.

If you can do this, you will be well-equipped for those days when you FEEL you can't bear your heartbreak, make anyone happy or do anything right. Challenging days will surely come and like David at Ziklag, (*1 Samuel 30:6*) you must be prepared to encourage yourself. In the midst of your confusion, complication or crisis, you will have to get up, stand up and speak a word over yourself. And you must do this, especially when you feel you *cannot* do it. It will take a little practice and you may want to rephrase or repackage my words, but I encourage you to take a few seconds each day to look in the mirror and just declare to yourself that you are enough.

Start by identifying any area, characteristic or circumstance that has ever made you feel inadequate. What is it? Family issues, body image and self-esteem, your neighborhood? It doesn't matter!!! Fill in the blank and practice now:

"I am _____ enough and I will make it." Now say it until you believe it because it is true. (*Romans 8:28-30 and Philippians 4:13*). Repeat this again the next day and the next.

If you master this or some version of this you will be prepared when negativity or crises arise and dare attack your very existence.

Once you are comfortable with the fact that you are enough, you will be ushered into the amazing revelation that not only are you enough but you are MORE than enough. You are the cup overflowing, a gushing, drenching waterfall, the manifested hopes and prayers of mothers, grandmothers and aunties, the bridge to the future.

You – just as you are today – are who we once were

You – are God's vision.

Dear Little Sista,

"Let's wait awhile" by Janet Jackson.

Those three words are the best advice I can give you with regard to your body, your sexuality.

Love and Sex are used interchangeable with regard to your body, but they hold two separate meanings and feelings.

Just because he said he loves you or you said that you loved him, is just not a good enough reason to share such a precious part of you, especially at this time and age of your life.
You are a treasure and worth the wait.

I use the word 'your' because you govern yourself. No one can determine your wealth and no one can take your precious jewels. You were born valuable; descendants of greatness and anything of value deserve and require the best.

I'm not here to preach but share with you what I experienced at this tender age. I thought it was love, I thought it was forever, the only thing that was forever was my daughter.
A responsibility that needed a grown and matured woman, not a love struck teenager.

So Little Sista, "Let's wait awhile" to share your precious jewels, because you're the real treasure.

Love,

Your Kim Maclin

How do you define your **TREASURES**:

_____

_____

_____

_____

_____

_____

_____

_____

_____

_____

_____

_____

_____

_____

_____

_____

_____

Dearest Little Sister,

The most important thing I want you to know as you travel life's journey is" God is able to do exceedingly abundantly above all you could ask or think" and

"God makes no mistakes." *According to Psalm 139: 13-14, you have been fearfully and wonderfully created gifts from God.* You are the apple of HIS eye.

Always remember,

"Lessons lived are Lessons Learned".

You must believe that on this journey of life, just because something doesn't work out the way you expected it to, doesn't mean it wasn't meant to happen that way. There is always a lesson in the experience. So, trust your natural instinct (that nagging feeling way down in the pit of your stomach). Trust God. Trust HIS Process. Then you will be able to keep your mind and heart open to the needless possibilities life has to offer you.

Love, Hugs & Kisses....

Always In His Grace and Service,

Teresa Johnson

I **TRUST** that God makes no mistakes today I will trust my instincts and walk in my gifts, I have many gifts and my gifts are:_____

_____
_____
_____
_____
_____
_____
_____
_____
_____
_____
_____
_____
_____

Dear Sister,

Reflection is the key!

I have been writing in my journal since the 8th grade. Without my journal, I wouldn't be the young woman that I am today! The stages from preteen to adulthood dealing with insecurities; not having many friends and being a lost soul. I have redefined ME! After writing in my journal year after year my feelings, goals, concerns, dreams, and questions I was already forming my identity as a YOUNG BLACK WOMAN. Though, every few years I always go back and reread my journal to seek how much I've grown and where I'm heading. I love writing my story! To you my SistaQueen, this poem is dedicated to you because you are your own best friend and there is nothing more prized than seeking self-awareness and unconditional self-love.

<u>My Best Friend</u>

My best friend never judged me

My best friend never criticized me

I was able to express myself fully and just be free

My best friend always took me to a place called "Utopia"

She took me to a fantasy where I was the only one there

She heard my cries

She felt my pain

She healed my heart

She filled my soul

Without her I wouldn't be the woman that I am today

She keeps reminding me where I come from and where I am going

She helps me make wise decisions

She calms me down when I'm upset

She opens up to me as much as I open up to her

She doesn't have to say a word and I listen soundlessly

Our relationship is reciprocated

She gives to me as much as I give to her

That's why she is my best friend

Because she is a reflection of ME

Who might my best friend be...MY JOURNAL

Written By: April V. Thomas

Dear Beautiful Starchild,

I want you to know that you are a wonderful unique being destined for greatness. On the road to greatness, destiny and your dream, you will find out that the path is difficult, especially now! There are so many people, places, things and ideas that will tell you that you are inadequate, incapable or even ignorant to the point that those nouns will make you feel inferior, inept and indecisive on moving toward your greatness. DO NOT ALLOW NOUNS TO TAKE AWAY YOUR DREAMS!

Starchild, you are going to constantly be surrounded by people. You will have those who will love you for who you are, and there will be those who will love you for what you can do or where you can take them. On the other hand, there will be people who just don't like you. Because our nature is curious, we would want to know why people just don't like you. Here is the answer: **They don't like you because you possess a quality that they don't have and want to acquire.** These are the people who will lie on you, talk about and make you feel bad about yourself- DO NOT LET THEM! These are your haters and they are such a small number that they do not matter. Turn your focus to those who love you. How do you know who is for you and against you? I am glad you have asked. I have some simple question I ask myself when dealing with people. The questions are: Is this person (people) healthy for my self-esteem? Will this person (these people) bring me closer to my dream? Will I have hell to pay being with this person (people)? Is this person I can take to someone's opinion I respect? If the answer is NO to any of these questions, then that person or people may not be needed in my life at this time. After a while, you will realize your haters and those who tag along because of who you are will fall off. Soon, you will become oblivious to who those people are or why they were significant.

Next Starchild, be weary of the places you go to and the institutions you attend. Every place is not a healthy place to go to or be in attendance. There will be places that will draw you out of your comfort zone and push you into your destiny. Knowing your path will eliminate the cause for you going places that will not aid in the building of your dream. A word of caution, there will also be places that will peak your interest, awaken your curiosity, and satisfy your need to be different. While you are there, ask yourself these questions: Is this place healthy for my self-esteem? Will this place bring me closer to my dreams? Will I have hell to pay being here? If the answer is NO to any of these questions, run like you have on lighted gasoline underwear and get away.

YOU MUST GET YOUR THINKING UNDER CONTROL! I purposefully put ideas and thoughts last because on your road to greatness you will be discourage and people will tell you NO! You will have your heart broken, things will exclude you and your ideas may be too great for others to fathom but in the interim, change your mindset. Tell yourself, "Today, I choose to believe that my dream will come into fruition!" You continue to tell yourself that until you achieve all that you aspire to have and dream.

As I close, I repeat do not allow nouns (people, places, things and ideas) get on your path for greatness and trip you up. You have so much to offer to this world! Love will come on your path. Being approved by others will come on this path. Being adored, needed and wanted will come on your path for greatness. While on your path, remember your goal and your questions that are listed above and you will not fall off the beaten path as much as you think. Forgive those who may not understand your path for they will come around once they see your greatness. Keep your thoughts positive. When an obstacle is encountered on your path, you will not have the wrong people to contend with, you will not be in the wrong place to get help, you will not have the wrong things in your vicinity and you will have the right ideas to keep you focused on the goal- your dream. I love you Starchild.

Your Big Sister,

Camesha

On my **PATH** to greatness I will stay positive and name my ideas, people I want in my life, places and things I want to see and do. I will be a Star, I **dream** of becoming...

_____
_____
_____
_____
_____
_____
_____
_____
_____
_____
_____
_____

On Redefining Beauty from a Mother's Perspective

Growing up might leave you with some scars sometimes. Don't let yourself feel bad about the scars you may feel on the inside or see on the outside. It just means that you survived some things! Did you know that even your mother's might feel a certain kind of way about themselves and may need to embrace their beauty? I know I did. As an adult, motherhood still challenged my self-image. I realized though that I define me, and my scars show strength.

As you read this piece, reflect and think about what you have overcome in your life. What shows your strength and beauty?

Stretch Marks... Where are your stretch marks?

Mine extend from one pelvic bone to the other

In the beginning, I noticed one line in my seventh month

Thought it was a scratch.

Joked darkly that our active baby boy

Had scratched me from the inside in an early attempt to get out on his own.

The sign of the single line

reminded me to faithfully apply concoctions of

Cocoa butters and creams

The eighth month of his head, hands & feet

pushing & prodding

the walls of my womb Woke me to new signs

He sought more freedom than his confines permitted

Limitations were the last thing I wanted for him

yet his first experience

Where are your stretch marks?

Mine extend from one pelvic bone to the other

In the ninth month

Skin stretched as he redefined his space in centimeters

of liberation

And I lost count as we grew together

Me to my heaviest weight

On that new end of the scale & Him to what would become his birth

weight to enter the world

Our shared growth tattooed itself just below my waistline

Life left lines cross my spirit

As my soul stretched to include

This new identity and pushed me past my emotional capacity

Where are your stretch marks?

Mine extend from one pelvic bone to the other

Visible lines tell tale

Of creation within my womb

Yet I am told to use cocoa butters & creams to remove them

Wipe them across my belly , Erase his cryptic calligraphy.

Companies create profits from chemical compounds

Created to produce Ambi cream amnesia

On our skin

Because what is the value of remembering our stories when there are just so

many products for sale to make us forget

Forget ourselves, Forget even our skin

Replace it with even skin smooth even skin

Smooth Like dolls, Even Like Barbie dolls

Fresh off the production line we buy the lines we are sold

About our bodies until even our skin is rewritten

Faces peer intently into mirrors

without seeing any original lines

Just those madeup from makeup

Now no longer a customer of concealers

I bought something better

& its priceless

Paid for in nights lying awake

Hands running over belly

Hands clasped

Praying his future & my past would join together to

Create family

I paid for each line in

Nights of pain and

Mornings of fatigue

I paid for each line

in carrying him to term

And a week beyond it

When he wasn't ready

And now I am not ready

or willing

to smear substances

As bleach

To treat his origin stories

Like stains

No, his story lines are too precious to be stripped of them.

So, instead, stripped down before the mirror I'll see his-story

Where are your stretch marks?

Mine extend from one pelvic bone to the other.

by Bella

No Makeup

I woke up this morning too tired to put on makeup.

But I have these blemishes, plus people know me by that beat

look....

I hesitate to grab the brushes; but I just don't have the energy

The energy to paint over who God already painted me to be

Why take out time to appear flawless when beneath the layers of

Mac you can't see my true blush,

Contouring and concealing, when I should be revealing

I'm hiding in the shadows of their shadows the real me, I

am a Cover Girl because the pictures say

perfection is key- but today forget all that; forget what

"they" say!

I DEFINE me!

Not my lipstick, not my liners,

Not my glosses or refiners

Just this freshly washed face that I see....

And it's naturally perfect to me.

By Keyona Bre'

Here I am

Hey Lil Sista,

Hi, how are you? It's so nice to meet you again. I know you're asking, "What makes me so nice to meet?" I'm not simple or naïve for asking "this" when others have forgotten that you exist.

I know parents should love and care for you no matter what, but when you needed them the most they were off living on their own, with dreams of never coming home.

Remember when they said, they would always have your back, but when things started to unravel, and you were unsure if you should fight back, or bend. They were only interested in, did you win.

Don't forget when they said, it just happened, but it won't ever again. So you looked forward and the excuses began. They said, it's a new day and not really about, THEN.

Could you have ever imagined that you would end up like that, leaking Abandonment and lack. You are not, what you have gone through or what has happened to you.

Here I am, standing before you, knowing what you've been thru. I see you and you are no longer abandoned, but bound with love, and cared for by sistafriends, and mothers again.

What makes you so different from the rest, is that I know you were formed from the best. Regardless of what you go through, God is with you.

Love your Sis,

Sherrie Williams-Rowe

My Dearest Little Sista,

How are you today? I have been thinking about you and wondering how are you getting along, before I get into my purpose of writing this letter to you I want to say thank you so much for still being here. Thank you so much for not taking your life when it seemed the only thing left to do to make the pain go away. I may not know you personally but in spirit I do and it would have broken my heart to see the news or read the newspaper to find that my little sista have left this world because she felt the pain was too strong or she felt that no one cared enough about her for her to stay around. You are my little sista and for that I love you dearly and I am so glad that you are here.

My purpose for writing you this letter is to say that it is ok, let me explain. Our bodies are sacred, it was a shell that God gave to us as a gift and it is left up to us to take care of it, your body is yours and it is special to you as it should be. The sad part about it is that sometime people may feel it is their right to take your gift, your body and do what they want to do with it, they violate one of the precious gifts that God gave to us and they feel like it's okay. But it's not okay, and when that happens it leaves us broken and confused and we are left with dealing with the outcome.

Sometimes the outcome is other people blaming you for something you did not cause nor had any control over at the time. Sometimes you deal with feeling you are worthless and that is why this thing happened to you or you felt like why did God allow this to happen to me, what did I do wrong for God to be mad at me and I am here to dispel all of those lies.

I was violated at a young age, I was blamed, I felt worthless and not special and I too wondered why did God allow this to happen to me? I am here to tell you little sista that IT IS NOT YOUR FAULT! You are not worthless and believe it or not God was there, He kept you when you didn't know that that is what He was doing.

Sometimes bad things happen to good people because God has a bigger plan for your life. See what happened was, the devil wanted to destroy you, the devil wanted to get rid of you because he knew how special of a person you were and is, and God said I need her and I am going to keep her because she is beautifully and wonderfully made, God told the devil that that is her body but her spirit belongs to me and I will protect her.

94

You see the amazing thing is, is that you are still here and the devil didn't want you to be around and he thought he could cause you to lose your mind or kill yourself and then you wouldn't be around to help another little sista out. God wants us to help each other and the devil doesn't. Bad things are going to happen but the trick is to not let the bad thing destroy you because that is what the devil wants and we don't want the devil to get any happiness out of hurting us.

God is **NOT MAD** at you; He loves you so much and He is so very proud of you for fighting your way back, you are so strong and so beautiful and such an outstanding young lady. It doesn't matter if you have done some things that aren't quite right, none of us are perfect we are going to make mistakes sometimes but we are all a work in progress. We are steady growing and we are steady learning and God forgives us for all of our mistakes if we ask Him too.

You don't have to cry about that bad thing that happened anymore because we are here praying for you in the spirit, I don't care what negative things someone may say to you please believe me when I tell you dear heart you are so very special, and even though I don't know you personally but I know your story, I love you so much and if I can love you like this never having the pleasure to have met you yet, can you imagine how much God loves you and He created you. You are the best thing that has happened in this world and never let anyone tell you any different.

I made it! At first I thought that I wouldn't and now I have the opportunity to share my story with you and I can tell you with truth and honesty that if I made it and I am walking in my purpose and my purpose is saving you then you can certainly do it too and save another sista friend just like you.

So go ahead baby girl and hold that beautiful head of yours up high show that wonderful smile of yours and know in your heart you got this! God is going to cover you and even when stuff happens he will not allow it to destroy you. God is going to use you to help someone else and it is such a beautiful feeling to know that you have helped someone else through a difficult time. I'm excited already to know that you are going to take this world by a storm and do something amazing. What I want you to remember always is this one important thing. I BELIEVE IN YOU!!!!!! And life would be boring without you in it.

Always and Forever
Your SistaKeeper for Life,
Reba R. Rice-Portwood

Now recite this prayer:

Dear God,
Since I am now free, it is my desire to forget those things
that lie behind and push forward to what lies ahead, I press
on toward the goal to win the [Supreme and Heavenly] prize
to which you in Christ Jesus are calling me upward. The past
will no longer control my thinking patterns or my behavior.
Praise be to You! I am a new creature in Christ Jesus. Old
things have passed away, and behold, all things have become
new. I declare and decree that henceforth I will walk in
newness of life.
Forgive me, Father, for self- hatred and self- condemnation. I
am your child, you sent Jesus that I might have life and have
it more abundantly, thank You for the blood of Jesus that
makes me whole and thank You so much Dear God for
loving me.

A Rites of Passage

As girls enter into womanhood differs in various cultures…. How will you define Reaching the Essence of your Development!
Here we offer you various cultural views of the initiation into womanhood…

There are places on the Earth where first blood is a cause for joy and womanhood a source of pride. There, girls receive presents and the whole community meets to feast, dance and celebrate new women in their tribe.

Girls' initiation is not only about ceremonies, it is the whole time of puberty – turning from girl into woman. Together girls learn what it means to be a woman. An important part of this process is learning from elder women.

In some cultures there is another important aspect of initiation ceremony for girls – a rejuvenation, rebirth of the whole community. With her first blood, a life-giving, creative force fills the girl. This force has no name, or it has some sacred name, for example for Navajo Indians it is *Changing Woman.*

Cree tribe

Adolescence is the time of learning and preparation. As a young girl prepares for puberty starting at ages 8, 9 they spend a part of each day with a specially selected Grandma representing the elders. She teaches them the origin story of the tribe, the story of First Woman, First Mother and the origins of Mother Earth. She teaches them what it means to become a woman, about changes in the body and the development of the psyche. Girls learn self-defense and practice it on the tribe's boys. They gain knowledge about herbs soothing pain and preventing pregnancy. When they are finally ready, they spend time alone, in cleansing lodges. Only after two years of such preparation they are accepted into the tribe as women. They are perceived as those becoming Mother Earth, fertile, capable of creating and giving life.

Africa

Pygmies in Africa thought that menstrual blood was a gift, accepted with joy and gratitude by the whole community. The girl went with her friends to Elima House. It was a special hut. An elderly woman from the tribe taught girls and prepared them to first Blood ceremony – Elima ceremony. The Elima ceremony, in which the whole community takes part, is very joyful. Girls learned women's songs and sang them loudly in the forest. After the ceremony there ensued two months of celebrations – meetings, feasts, dances.

Nootka tribe - Initiation for girls is an important celebration for the whole tribe. After her first menstruation a big party is thrown for the girl and later comes an endurance ritual, during which she is taken far from the shore, into the sea and she must return alone, swim back to the shore. The whole village is waiting for her. From that moment on she has the rights of a grown woman.

"Sankofa" teaches us that we must go back to our roots in order to move forward. That is, we should reach back and gather the best of what our past has to teach us, so that we can achieve our full potential as we move forward. Whatever we have lost, forgotten, forgone or been stripped of, can be revived, preserved and reclaimed.

Now what do you experience when you experience menstruation in a freeway, not burdened with cultural prejudices?

1. Flow. On the physical, most direct level women experience flow – your blood flows freely throughout your body. You feel a small river, a stream from inside your bellies flowing down, towards the earth. A unique, specific sensation, particularly strong when we get up from bed after a night's sleep, or from a sofa when we've been sitting for a long time. We can feel like the Earth, from which – from the source - a River flows. Maybe this is the reason why the source has always been one of the most powerful symbols of femininity. If we accept this flow as a healthy pattern, it can become part of our other life experiences. Free flow of feelings, emotions, dreams. Life in the flow – not squeezed, not blocked, without corks or stoppers. Not dry, sterile but flowing, living, open new experiences, people, sensations.

2. Regeneration. Many women need a lot of sleep, a lot of rest while menstruating. They need to regenerate. During this time of month our body, our psyche craves relaxation. We cannot be active all the time – this is our body's lesson. In nature we have day and night. At night we sleep and dream – dream the future. Menstruation is our night. The time to slow down. Rest. Cherish ourselves.

3. Wisdom. During menstruation, especially on the first, second day, women seem absent, unconscious in a specific way. They find it hard to concentrate on facts, people, and actions. When you stop fighting with it, when you let yourself immerse in this state, you will experience an inward draw - inside your inner world.

If you lie down and close your eyes you may feel, hear, and see. It feels as if you were COILING UP inside, into the center like a snake, like a spiral, like a piece of thread.

Menstruation is the time of contact with the wisdom which lives inside us, the time when answers to important questions come - if we make space and time for this inward travel.

4. Energy. Women who don't ignore their cycle and work less just before menstruating and take time off in the first two days of their period often experience an exceptional energy flow. Vibrant, flowing energy is "spinning" or "dancing" inside their body – a unique, highly pleasant state.

5. Transition. Menstruation is the time of our cycle when our body experiences passage of time, death. The lining of endometrium in the uterus dies and, together with blood, leaves the body. It's our internal "new moon" – the time of an end and a new beginning.
Women who celebrate their cycle can naturally synchronize with this rhythm. During menstruation they take time for themselves and ask questions: What doesn't serve life anymore? What has become old, useless, what wants to pass away, disappear from my life? Which feelings, emotions, patterns have served their purpose, run their course? Then they make an intention – let them pass. And they let it happen...

After menstruation, when the time to act in the world comes, they introduce the changes into their lives. Thus, menstruation can become the time of good endings, planning changes. Making space for the new – new feelings, relations, and patterns. A time to let go and let life flow…

As you Reach your Essence of Development

WE want to offer you 8 RED keys to being

a Keeper to Self!

8 RED Keys to finding your Strength, Courage & Wisdom

Eight is the number for new beginnings, and as you enter into adolescence to adulthood. Your essence of development will be tested. As you begin to define your journey, we need you to know that no one has all the answers to life. This is a trial and error process, but you can learn from your mistakes and you must! You must keep moving forward, staying strong knowing who holds the key to your destiny. We all have choices but we must listen to that still voice inside that will not compete for attention but will always be ready to share when you can embrace the stillness of listening…

1.   I Choose. Many times in life you will be influenced to make difficult decisions. Which means you will have to think through what is next for yourself. Remember to always pray on it first! Seek advice from a trusted adult in your life, a counselor, sister or family member. You may be in unchartered territory, doing something you have never done before or no one else has ever done before. This decision can influence the rest of your life. So when you choose, please do not choose out of fear, always choose having faith knowing you are always becoming! It is your journey so you choose which direction you will go! It takes *Courage* but you can do it!

2.   I Define Me. Remember; who is the author of your story. No it is not music that defines you, television or social media, but the original author is GOD. He has a purpose for your life much bigger than you could ever imagine, but you must begin with the end in mind. So write out your personal mission, vision and allow the universe to gift you with details. Be patient. It will be the best gift you shall ever receive.

3. **Let your light Shine.** Know that you are simply beautiful, but beauty starts on the inside. It is definitely important to take care of yourself physically but be conscious of the words that come out of your mouth without filters. Once you make a statement be clear it is out of love and remember someone is always watching you. So stay humble. You don't have to be the first in a picture or to be in front of a camera for people to see you. You should shine naturally!

4. **Have an intimate relationship with God.** Speak to him every day, find a connection to a spiritual family to worship with, read and know the word. So when at your weakest moments you know where to seek your *Strength!*

5. **Know "This too shall pass."** Know that life will gift you with lessons and you must take the bitter with the sweet. Remember the Serenity prayer. God grant me the serenity to accept the things I cannot change, the knowledge to change the things I can and the *wisdom* to know the difference. Valleys come and go, but if you have God you will be able to keep climbing, turn down a different path and reach your mountaintop.

6. **Be a Voice.** Listen to your voice be honest with yourself. Allow your voice to take a stand for injustices and to be a leader, but remember to stay humble and never surround yourself around YES girls! You know what I am saying; the type of girls that won't challenge you to grow. Friends should have similar moral values and boundaries. Remember that birds of a feather flock together so be a good friend to yourself and your sista. If you must share your secrets, sometimes it is best to write it in your personal journal. Being a keeper to self is a necessity. Never allow someone to take your voice, your voice defines your character, when you speak others will listen. Your words matter. Maya Angelou once said, "I've learned that people will forget what you said, people will forget what you did, but people will never forget how you treat them.

7. **Know your worth.** Remember if a person comes into your life then they are here for two things, to give or to take. So you must take note if they are an asset or a debit. If they are a debit they are no credit to you, therefore you must withdraw. Always sow positive seeds into your life! Remember real love will wait. In this microwave society we are in the "I want it now" era. Be a Keeper of your values, facebook, instagram and any online outlet that cost you in the future. When you say NO mean it! Have the *courage* to stand up for what you believe in. Remember sex does not equal love, so by all means if you can stay pure until marriage; make it a goal to pursue purity. If you find this goal difficult for you, make an adult decision and protect yourself at all times and remember you are a gift from God so treasure yourself.

8. **OWN your NOW!** We cannot express enough to walk in your destiny, do the things you love, things that you are led to do and start now with a plan. Don't be afraid of change, meet new people, step out of your comfort zone, laugh outloud, be bold and create your tomorrow, by owning your today and knowing that having **strength, courage and wisdom** is an inside job so own it! Thanking God daily for allowing you to celebrate your life today!

"Except for God"

Pre-Scriptures for the Soul...

In Life you will need affirmations that will give you the Strength, Courage and wisdom to make it through. You may love music, meditation, talking to a close friend, walking in the park or sitting alone in your favorite sacred spot. Regardless of the many options you may have to soothe your spirit in times of experiencing growing pains which you will endure. You must know that God almighty has the ultimate plan for you.

So here are a few scriptures to choose from; chosen just for you....

Trust in the lord with all your heart, and do not rely on your own understanding, think about him in all your ways, and he will guide you own the right paths. Proverbs 3:5-6

We love because He first loved us. 1 John 4:19 Live the way the Lord your God has commanded you so that you may live and know what is good. Deuteronomy 5:33

He shall teach us His ways and we shall walk in his paths. Isaiah 2:3

There is no wisdom, understanding, or advice that can succeed against the lord. Proverbs 21:30

Wherever your treasure is, there your heart and thoughts will also be. Luke 12:34

You will know the truth, and the truth will set you free. John 8:32

"No one has ever seen, no one has ever heard, no one has ever imagined what God has prepared for those who love him." 1 Corinthians 2:9

Walk by Faith, not by sight 2 Corinthians 5:7

Be a Keeper!

K -Keeper to thyself first,

E -Enlighten yourself by reading, listening & journaling,

E -Engage others by sharing information

P -Purpose driven girls reach their destiny

E -Empower another sista to be a Keeper

R -Respect yourself, reflect and reach your essence of development

Giving honor to all of The Red Book

Nia Sista Keeper Contributors

(Women who are truly Keepers in the Community)

In honor of JaMeah Echols

As you begin to leave the chapters behind and begin to write your own story! We leave you all with a letter JaMeah wrote me before she transitioned! She is always with us! A Keeper for Life!

Know that God has given you a Keeper! Whether they are here in the physical or in the spirit! JaMeah We miss you! SK4Life! You truly are a RED girl! You have reached your Essence of Development! Peace Within!

A SKisUaSKisMEaSKisWE!

Tracie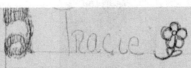

You are what's been missing in my life, you have taught me things I would've probably learned the hard ways ever since I came a sistakeeper my life has changed. I have been through slumps but I've learned 2 love myself 1st then others, which has helped me with some of my biggest problems.

What you do is great and you are a blessing, I consider you as a second mother by your teachings and what you've done 4 me. Even my mom says the same! I am so thankful for all you've done, especially the trip last week 2 Nashville. It was a great experience and I am so glad I went because I learned a lot and the conference helped me realize some things and just being with everyone was fun, even though we changed hotels, I think it was still fun because more of us could stay in the same room. Well, even though I don't speak 2 you about my problems you somehow answer them in the little sistakeeper sessions and @ free your mind fridays♡ maybe we have a connection that is still being discovered. I mean I have never been able 2 accept anyone's words because I like 2 be right but when you speak I listen and I continue 2 listen, which isn't normal 4 me because I probably remember everything you've said but I barely remember what I said 2 my friends yesterday♡ Anyway~ I know I don't speak a lot but it's because I hold things in, but as you can see I haven't been as quiet and I think I can let a little more out♡ so thank you 4 helping me 2 realize how special I am and thanks 4 filling that empty space in my life♡ which was you♡ you R my sistakeeper♡

Thanks 4 everything♡ @lways

113

A SistaKeeper is You!

A SistaKeeper is me!

A SistaKeeper is WE!

A SistaKeeper is You!

A SistaKeeper is me!

A SistaKeeper is WE!

A SistaKeeper is You!

A SistaKeeper is me!

A SistaKeeper is WE!

Tracie Berry-McGhee, M. Ed, NCC, LPC

(DivineTea)

Tracie Berry-McGhee, poetically speaking (DivineTea) received her Bachelor of Arts in Psychology in 1990 and her M. Ed in counseling, in 1998 from the University of Missouri, St. Louis.

In 2003, she produced a spoken-word CD, and self-published SistaKeeper Poetry for the Soul Chapbook, curriculum and journal for young girls seeking to find self, and become aware of their purpose. In 2004, SistaKeeper Empowerment Center became a nonprofit organization in St. Louis, MO and now has chapters in Africa, Jamaica, New Mexico and Germany. The goal is nurturing inner awareness, building self-esteem and developing purpose in girls and women. In March 2005, she started her private practice Imani Counseling & Consulting Services, specializing in women and teen girl issues.

Today, she serves as Executive Director of SistaKeeper Empowerment Center and founder of The Nia Group STL, a wellness center for women where she currently provides individual counseling, facilitates circles and promotes young women finding their purpose through motivational speaking engagements in local, national, and global communities. She speaks on topics such as conflict resolution, dealing with low self-esteem, and bullying, releasing anger through her creative expressions, use of bibliotherapy and poetry-based curriculum. As a dynamic speaker, therapist, and consultant through her continuous commitment Tracie Berry-McGhee, has demonstrated her dedication to diversity and the empowerment of young women today. She is a member of Delta Sigma Theta Sorority Inc, St. Louis Metropolitan Alumnae Chapter, Member of Christ the King, UCC and native of St. Louis, Missouri. Tracie is the wife of Nathaniel McGhee and the proud mother of three beautiful children: Khalia, Bria, and Nathaniel. Most importantly a child of GOD!

For booking information visit

www.niagroupstl.com

This Red Book Journal

Belongs to

_____

123

Made in the USA
Las Vegas, NV
14 August 2024

93829845R00079